The baby o

By Beverley Randell

Illustrated by Elizabeth Russell-Arnot

Down on the farm
the cows are asleep.

The pigs are asleep.

The dogs are asleep.

3

Up in the tree
the owls
are **not** asleep.

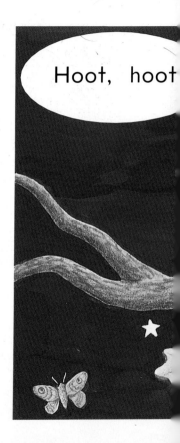

Hoot, hoot

The baby owls

are hungry.

Mother Owl
is looking for moths.

Mother Owl
sees a big moth.

Here comes
Mother Owl!

9

Mother Owl
comes to the tree.

The big moth
is for the baby owls.

Hoot, hoot!
Hoot, hoot!

Down on the farm
the cows are asleep.

The pigs are asleep.

The dogs are asleep.

Up in the tree
the baby owls
are asleep, too.